Live
Oak
Poems of Texas

Elizabeth Anne Hin

Copyright © 2016 Elizabeth Anne Hin

All Rights Reserved

Illustrations Copyright © 2016 by Cynthia L. Kirkwood

Editing and Design by Sarla V. J. Matsumura

Library of Congress Control Number: 2016907044

ISBN-13: 978-0692582770
ISBN-10: 0692582770

Printed in the United States of America

Published by Issa Press
Austin, Texas

DEDICATION

To my Family

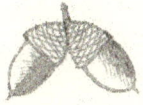

CONTENTS

Texas	1
Crawfish	3
That's That	5
Cattle Drive	9
Hard to Say	11
Texans	13
Yankee Poem	15
Texas Woman	17
Good Old Boys	19
Texas Pecan-Sized	21
Brothers	23
Your Honor	27
Joshua	31
Cruel Texan	35
W	37
John Pierce	39
Steve	41
In Texas	43
Birdsong	45
Spanish Oak	55
Enchanted Rock	57
My Texan	59
Across that Texas Sky	61
Fifth Child	63

TEXAS
It was
not
the Alamo
that
defined Texas
for this Yankee
where everyone died
and a great hole of tragedy
carved itself irreparably
into the memory of the Texas soul
into the limestone of the building
into the slow conscious growing of the roots and
cells of the Live Oak trees
at her wellspring.

It was
the San Jacinto
where
in eighteen minutes
the Texans said
no.
Just like this
Yankee.

No one
will ever be
remembered
into eternity
for doing this to us.

We will
be
Who
and what
That Great One
created
us to be
in eternity
not through any scar
but
through the
majesty
and the mystery
of the One
who created
the Enchanted Rock
the whispering stone
the holy place
of the Comanche.

Who upon that
rock
made abiding
peace
with the Yankees
of Texas.

CRAWFISH

Texas
You stick in my craw
You old Southern fish
You just don't care
  about anything
  'cept yourself.

No other state
  is like this
  because
  every other state
  cares.

About everyone.
Even Texans.

THAT'S THAT

He said you're from the North
She said you're from the South
He said why don't you doctor like me
She said why don't you watch your mouth
I doctor all kinds of souls
With my loving heart
Including yours, Big Texan
That was so sad and proud
He said I've loved before
And I don't need you
But, well, you can stay.
And that's that.

He took her dancing
Down at the Gruene Hall.
She'd seen the world, you know
Boy, she'd seen it all
Every continent
But with his boots, his heart
His shining Texan eyes.
Well, that's that.

He took her walking
Out on his Daddy's land
They talked of Fireflies, Flowers, and olden days.
They ate at Kreitz Barbecue
Drove back home amid Bluebonnets
That's that.

He was from Texas
She was from the North
They had disputes
About what life was about
And after talking and
Listening too
They said
Well Darling, that's that.

She called her Darling
and he was silent
She made him dinner
And he was still
She took his arm
And walked beside him
Down in Texas
I guess that's that.

She was a Northern girl
He didn't like it
She spoke her heart and mind
And he did, too.

She came from New York
He came from Texas
There was a showdown
I guess you'd say that

She put her boots on
He said let's rodeo
She said it's Austin
He said I guess that's that.

She said
    I miss my trees
    all golden in the field
    quietly in the breeze
    the sky above it all
He said
    we have Spanish Oak
    turning copper in the Winter
    then he was still
    as only a Texan man can be

And she said
I guess that's that.

She said
    I miss the ocean
    the lake
    the rivers
    the city
    the South
    the North
    the East
    the West.

And he said
That's all right.
And stood beside her
as many a Texan man can do
She sighed
and was content
and one
and he said
I guess that's that.

CATTLE DRIVE

I don't know
You Texas men
You better show me
Some of your best moves.
So far
All I've seen
Is rope her up
Draw her in
Tie her down
Brand her

Breed her
Feed her
Bathe her
Douse her
She's alright
For a heifer
Got her at a good price.

HARD TO SAY

It's hard to say
   What Texans think about Yankees
They say
   How dee (Howdy)
   How'r y'ew (How are you)
   I herd 'bout yew (I heard about you)
   Yer ta one kin tell ta futur (You're the one can tell the future)

They betray their wives
   Daughters-in-law, friends, colleagues,
   Clients
And hold up
That the old boy with the money
   And cruelty
   And the lies
Is the boss
   In Texas.
Not like any Yankee I know.
Four years here in Austin.

TEXANS

You Texans
You all say
You're from
The North
So what
You all aren't from
Somewhere
Too
Each one's place different
And

Don't we all cherish
Enchanted Rock
Cypress over
The azure Guadalupe
Blue Northers
Rolling in
So high
In that broad sky
Their color
Mood
Wind off
The Gulf
Up across Austin
All year
Many Oaks
Live, Post
And Spanish

Turning burnished copper
Like nothing else
Anywhere

And
Lady Bird's
Many wildflowers
Every day
All year
In the fields
And the byways
Of our Texas

YANKEE POEM

Texas
you can spit
better than
anyone I know.

But I
can kiss
better than you.

TEXAS WOMAN

I.

Texas woman

Vixen

Seductress

How much money

Does he have

Does he make

I want it all

I'll just pretend

I want him

Do I love him?

Isn't that what I just

Told y'all?

II.

Texas woman

Tough, tough

Vixen

No

Just cunning

Seductress

Always

Premeditated

For self

Like her Texas

Counterpart

In men

How much money
How much land
How many things
And how important
And how much
And how important
Does he have
Does he make
I want it all
I'll just pretend
I want him
Do I love him?
Isn't that what
I just
Told all y'all?

GOOD OLD BOYS

They were Texans.
You know, just good old boys.
They were not good men.

One I know liked to count his money
Drink expensive vodka, too much;
And then come in for the kill.
Another, family doctor, physician, practitioner,
Promised, "Do not harm," you know, from Hippocrates;
His oath, pledged by all allopaths, regarded everyone,
Except his wife, her children, her friends, her dying
    mother,
And everyone I know.

I would not be with them
When they meet God.

They're Texans.
You know, just good old boys:
"Conquer her, destroy her."
Take all her ability to live, to thrive.
She was, is, and seems
Ever will be
Property
To you,
Because it's all property;
And it's all yours.

The very oil spits you out
The very soil
You good old boys
And girls
As something poisonous
To the soul of Texas.

TEXAS PECAN~SIZED

His penis was so small
That when his second wife walked out the door
He beat her to a pulp
With money
Lies
Neglect
And took his tiny penis
And his tiny soul
Away to another state
And left Texas and his former wife
To rest.
Let's have some pecan pie
And celebrate.

BROTHERS

I saw them
Riding up on the light ridge
The pale limestone outcropping
You know
Near the Spanish Oak
The one
That Northern girl of John David's
Loves so much
How it turns deep
Copper
In the soft
Texas Winter
She says.

I was leading them
I said
Jack
Tighten that girth
For Ernestine
You old cowboy
Like you would've
Once
When she was young
The age you first met
How
You would've done
Something
Anything

To stand against her
Doing a chore
Pretending it needed deep doing
'Cause it probably did
And you could touch her
With no more
Than your gesture
Needing to be said.

That day she wore
The peach dress
Cut out embroidery
Like my grandmother
Used to do at her kitchen
Table
John's girl calls it
Cutwork, tatting
So pretty
Curls and open face
That tiny spitfire
Made you a wife
And a home
And a beautiful
Daughter
A cowgirl to boot.

Well, now,
Get on, partner
Cause I'm taking you to witness
Her in Heaven
Just as Lanelle and I did
On our porch and
Home
That very fine day
You were wed.
It was fine.
Brother.

In honor of John Pierce Gabriel and Jack E. Gabriel

YOUR HONOR

I.
Outside
Marjorie's kitchen,
The daughter who bakes
Like your wife,
Whom you adored
But did not say,
Oklahoma Texan;

The tree
You so lovingly
Planted,
For her,
Japanese Maple,
Is in bud.

In bud after you
Lost that wife,
In an illness so long
And difficult,
It breaks my heart.

And you lost your judgeship,
Taking a few drinks,
To be with the emptiness you felt now

Beside you,
Forty some years of her
Beside you,
Privately beloved,
Somehow gone.

Hell, yesterday,
They simply shot
A judge,
In Atlanta;
No thank you, Your Honor,
No tree,
There.

No thank you, Your Honor,
No tree,
Here,
For your years of service,
Of careful, of difficult
Place it in the hands . . .
At the soul-tearing
Arguments of lawyerships,
At the husbanding,
The fathering,
The gardening.

Tree in bud
At your elder daughter's window;
Plant a tree
For her now,
Too,
Deep in your heart.

II.
At her kitchen window
Where she will bake,
Your heart will be held,
And mine,
Those of her three children
Those of others whom she loves,
By the tree,
By the pie,
So like her late
Beloved Mother,
Her Oklahoma Texan Mother,
Devotee of The Bible,
Of Autobiography of a Yogi, for God's sake,
Of deep consciousness and love.

Thank you, Your Honor.
Get up now.
Be at that bench
Of God's ethics.
We need you:
Father,
Grandfather,

Beloved friend,
Husband still;
Alive to be
A good,
Deep and true man,
Like a Japanese Maple,
Or an Austin Red Bud,
Or a Willow,
Or an Oak,
Your Honor.

What kind of pie shall we have?
Which one of her recipes,
She who will ever be
Beside you, now.

For Charles R. McClure

JOSHUA

We gathered
Memorialized you
On Red Bud Island
Red Buds full in bloom
Dogs all about
We stood for you
In a circle
At the end
Joshua.

You fell down
Pretty well
Heroin in your veins
Tattooed locks over those joints
Drinking, drinking
Even I cry at this now
But you
Got up
Joshua.

These last years
Of your life
You got up
Joshua.

Texas tough
Austin cool
Passion
And the deepest
Most profound
Penetrating love
Always
In your splendid face
You challenger of life
Sometimes kind
Sometimes collected
Like a cool dispassionate wind
Across the Hill Country
Across the worlds you knew
In the freedom of your skateboard
Your snowboard
Your journeys
You fierce, liberated soul
Of courage and of God
Joshua.

Tobacco anoints your body
As it now burns
Holy oil
Cedar: the death blessing of the Masons
Blue corn flour
Well-beloved skateboard board
Family quilt, brown and cream
Flowers
Candles

Prayers
Hymns
Poems
An altogether brilliant new tattoo: "Lucky"
At the right wrist
Joshua.

You were
On a quest
For the
Holy Grail
You have
Found her
And
She has found you
Eternity
Bandit, catch the ball
Joshua
Joshua.

For Joshua Bailey Rule and Family

CRUEL TEXAN

His Sadistic Texan wife
Turned into a brown recluse
Tried to bite all
Her friends
And ended up
Poisoning herself
Heart rotting
No God for her
Stuck on
Her own idea
Of what a
Texan is and
Should be
In eternity
Sad
Texas rejects her.

W

People love you; people hate you.
You're a Yankee Texan.
Clearing cedar: dirty, bark scorpions, dust, sap, a few
    snakes.
The dog's alright.
That beautiful, penetrating Texas wind across the land.
Clearing your head.
Driving all over The Hill Country: winter rain, spring
    flowers, summer balm, autumn deer; just everything
    about it.
Stop for pie.
Papers in Washington: decisions, meetings, dinners, nice
    suit, good shoes, a kiss to Laura.
Early to bed.
Men killed: the Bible at your side early morning, prayers
    for every one of those men, prayers for every
    human being on every side, every way, every nation,
    "On Earth as it is in Heaven."
And courage: faith in, hope for, and love enough to
    embody, what is your will today, Lord,
In Texas,
Everywhere.

For George Walker Bush

JOHN PIERCE

It was John Pierce
Who called me
John Pierce
Was a Mason
He called out to me

He drove a truck
Loved his wife
And raised
A most precious
Only son

He had
A pet goat
For eighteen years
Strong asthma
And a great heart
Cattle, and so many stories

He told me
You are safe into eternity
Upon my land

Near the Alamo
Near the Piney Woods
Near the hills, near the creeks
Which called me
By name
To remember
You are his son's beloved

Come here
To Texas now.

STEVE

Get on over here
You good lookin' cowboy
About as good looking
As my bearded Texan

Got to saddle up her horse
Don't you know a cowgirl
When she's grieving
Her Mama

She said I'm fine

And taking her up on the ridge
The pale limestone ridge
That balm wafts in from the Gulf
And sweeps softly over the land
Just as the day she was born
And conceived
Their only one

And she sees the trees
Springing to bud
And a calf across the way

And she is fine

And her Mama
Remembers
When she met you

Ah, that's just like
When I met my Jack

My cowgirl will be
Just fine
With him riding beside
her

Get on up there
On your two horses
Then stay there
You heard her Mama

For Joanie Marie Gabriel

IN TEXAS

Last eve
I drove
With our little one
To the post office
To mail a letter
To a beloved poet

A few miles
From our home
Up on the Rochelle overpass
Above 114
My breath
Went away
It truly
Went away

For there
They were
Bluebonnets
First of this season

My breath came back
In Texas

BIRDSONG

My Texan
Placed a birdfeeder
With his great care.

He hoped
I would not miss
my Desert Wren
Mourning Doves
Great Horned Owls
Blue Heron
Hawks
Tanagers
Gambrell's Quail
Hummingbirds
Sparrows
and songbirds
too much.

Well
since last winter
near his North Texas home
I have met
Cormorants
Sparrows
Grackles
Robins
Finches
red and yellow.

Cardinals
Egrets
Great Blues
Lesser Blues
Herons
that is
my Mother's bird

And my favorite
A Kingfisher
who perches upon
telephone wire and such
fishing and sunning
in the morns
on the way
to the Darlings' school.

I love him
he makes me completely
inutterably happy.

Sometimes
I turn
the car around
and visit with him
for a bit
him upon his wire

me with the car heater on
and the window rolled down
having a Kingfisher conversation
in North Texas.

The Kingfisher
the bird who is to announce
like Archangels
that
Jesus is here.

He lets me know
this
every time
I am gifted with him
Upon his wire.

One morn
there were birds
in the grey sky
of North Texas
so cold
this winter
several hundred
tawny burnished
Cardinal cousins

females
migrating
ensemble
that is
together.

They arrived
in the sky
offering
a tender Texas visit
a Southern visit
genteel, warm
conversational
and true
at our bedroom window.

It was
the first time
I did not miss
my Desert Wren
more than I could stand.

They were not
homesick
my birds
of Texas
they called
to me
with color
songs

movement
and the
very sweetest spirit.

I came right
to the garden door
I could not stay away
I returned
to that threshold
seven times.

They were
a veritable wonder.

I drew my breath
and I sighed
in beauty
that cold
and grey
North Texas day.

I opened
the garden door
and stood
in the chill
in the muted charcoal sky
of the late morn
to be with them
they welcomed me
from several feet away

on bricks
pillars
shrubs
trees
nibbling
chirping
drinking
from patio puddles
very near me
and
with one another
so completely.

This entire winter
for which
my sister friend
of Texas
with the deepest
sweet drawl
apologized
a few days later.

She said
Honey, I'm so sorry
your first
North Texas winter
she said
well, the cold
was alright
that's nothing

but the sky
is never grey
almost
the sky
is almost always
like that
right up there
today
winter's pretty
much gone
now anyway
you shouldn't worry about it.

I didn't.

She wasn't finished.

First North Texas winter
ever like this one
her fiftieth year
upon this earth
never seen one like this
well.

Besides
you look good
peaceful.

A large tree was filled with birds
Such a myriad of colors

a wonder of songs
that I stopped
before entering our car
for errands
yesterday.

I turned
like a beloved Sufi friend
turning in her Dervish dance for God
to regard them
in the trees
beside the house
maybe thirty
varied species
I will have to purchase
a book
the lovely one
I found
at Fort Worth
to name them
so we can visit
properly
introduced.

They look good
peaceful

Many colors
many birdsongs
they tell me the saints are here
of all faiths
with Jesus
in North Texas
at my Texan's home.

(The "Cardinal cousins" are Cedar Waxwings and Pyrrhuloxias.)

SPANISH OAK

At a routine checkup at a famous hospital in Houston
He, of Lebanon, said to me
In late November on my birthday, forty-ninth
Prepare your family
Maybe six months, a year
You roll up your sleeves and I'll roll up mine
I'll see you in January
In Houston
He, of Mexico, placed needles deep into my throat
Stoic and caring, as tears ran down my cheeks
He said to me, heal yourself like a shaman
In Houston
He, of some ancestral birth blue-eyed like a Northern Scot
Opened my throat
In Austin
She, of Zimbabwe, Rhodesia then, like Mr. Tipler who has
    the best lamps on the planet, on Fifth Street
Gave me medicine of pharmacy, food, exercise, art, life,
    love, kabbalistic prayer
Like that of her noble Austrian father, saving them all
    from the ovens of war
In the Hill Country
He, another son of Lebanon's Cedars
Opened my womb, probing, looking, counseling
His wife was from Austin

My life flows through their grace like the sap
    of a Live Oak tree
Or the Spanish Oak along Hamilton Pool Road turned
    copper, ochre, shimmering in late autumn, tinted like
    my soul now that I have lived to be a Texan
Like him of Lebanon, like him of Mexico, like him
    of Scottish heritage, like her with a life of blessing,
    like him, hands birthing babies, hands birthing elders,
    like me
Branches turning to new bud and leaf.

For Dr. Ridha Arem
Dr. Souhail Asfouri
Dr. John David Gabriel
Dr. Michael Stewart
Dr. Margaret Well
And Mr. Neil Tipler

ENCHANTED ROCK

O rock
of Comanche peace
you who hold
our continent safe
in a blessing
of German Yankees
and Native peoples of the original continent

Who all
prayed
on the rose face
of your great body
and from this place
sent out a
prayer

I feel
I know
today.

You are the
peace of
the holy pipe
of the Native American people
embodied
in my heart,
here in Texas
and everywhere.

MY TEXAN

The Cottonwoods
were budding
along the Verde River
the day I knew
you would cherish
me forever

I headed North
to Hotevilla
to greet the Kachinas
come down from
the mountains to
bless us

You, at the
office, hospital
blessing your
many children

with your loving care
my Texan.

ACROSS THAT TEXAS SKY

Across that
Texas sky, his soul
Poured itself,
Like a sunset.
Or a sunrise.
That day had begun
His day began
His name was John
His name, John.

FIFTH CHILD

If we had a son
a Texas star

shooting across the Milky Way
to our souls
and our mature bodies
God would call him Bowie

He would cradle our aging hearts
like a great knife
cutting apart all the ends of humanity's true decline

unafraid of the universe
standing beyond the Alamo

for truth and
all that is great

Bowie, John Bowie
this works for me
works for God,
Texan.

ACKNOWLEDGEMENTS

Many thanks to the Editors of the following publications in which poems were previously published: Austin International Poetry Festival, *Di-verse-City Anthology, 2016,* "Enchanted Rock;" and Dos Gatos Press, *Texas Poetry Calendar,* "Yankee Poem."

ABOUT THE AUTHOR

Elizabeth Anne Hin studied poetry formally with George E. Dimock, Richard Wilbur, William Hoover Van Voris, Michael Benedikt, Elizabeth Hardwick, Sir Stephen Spender, and Joseph Brodsky. Her Mother read poetry aloud from *A Child's Garden of Verses* by Robert Louis Stevenson and from other cherished texts from Beth's conception through childhood. Her Father taught her through his admiration for Homer's life, work, and virtuous message, from the world's classics and histories, and from noble and heroic peoples and cultures of all nations. He practiced his faith in the equality of all men and women, and in all aspiration: 'Ad astra per aspera,' ~Seneca. Her Mother was a private living example of this virtue.

Beth has embraced poetry, from reading to writing, since youth, observing in gratitude the poetry infused in sculpture at Wellington's port in New Zealand and attending readings by Jorge Luis Borges at the 92nd Street YMCA in Manhattan, New York, Adrienne Rich in a hallowed hall of Amherst, Massachusetts, Drummond Hadley and Gary Snyder in Anchorage, Alaska, Mary Oliver at a Presbyterian Church in Dallas, Texas. She has been shown kindness in mentoring by writers from John Updike to Carlos Fuentes, Richard Erdoes to Derek Walcott; and by W. S. Merwin, who expressed to her in 1973 that he had written nearly every day since the age of 21, and requested of Beth that she do the same.

ALSO BY ELIZABETH ANNE HIN

The Grail: A Story of Issa and Yeshua, 2014

Jdg: Poems of Love, 2016

Willow: Poems of Devotion, 2016

Published by Issa Press, Austin Texas

www.ingramcontent.com/pod-product-compliance
Lightning Source LLC
Chambersburg PA
CBHW022120090426
42743CB00008B/933

* 9 7 8 0 6 9 2 5 8 2 7 7 0 *